For Sophie, and all her fabulous furry friends! —K. H.

To everybody who loves their pup! —L. C.

Farrar Straus Giroux Books for Young Readers
An imprint of Macmillan Publishing Group, LLC
120 Broadway, New York, NY 10271 · mackids.com

Our books may be purchased in bulk for promotional, educational, or
business use. Please contact your local bookseller or the Macmillan
Corporate and Premium Sales Department at (800) 221-7945 ext. 5442
or by email at MacmillanSpecialMarkets@macmillan.com.

Library of Congress Cataloging-in-Publication Data is available.

First edition, 2022
Book design by Lisa Vega
Color separations by Embassy Graphics
Printed in China by Toppan Leefung Printing Ltd., Dongguan City,
Guangdong Province

ISBN 978-0-374-38919-2 (hardcover)
10 9 8 7 6 5 4 3 2 1

WHAT'S UP, PUP?

How Our
Furry Friends
Communicate
and What They
Are Saying

KERSTEN HAMILTON   PICTURES BY LILI CHIN

Farrar Straus Giroux · New York

When you and your buddy go out for a **walk,**

watch **very** closely—
you'll see your pup talk!

Dogs talk with their **waggers**

and **sniffers**
and **ears.**

They talk
with their
muzzles,

their
eyes,

and their **rears.**

In
Hong Kong

or New York, **wherever** you go,

dogs politely look away
before they say **hello**.

Eyes soft and blinking,

a wag—perhaps wide—

then dogs who are meeting

approach from the side.

Next, pretty purebreds, mixes, or mutts

must **wuffle-whiff** fur and **snuffle-sniff** butts.

Some dogs use paws and noses to point—

Look at that!

While stiff legs and hard stares say,

This scratch means
I'm nervous.

That yawn says,
I'm wary. I want to feel safe, and bath time is scary!

A front strrrrreeeetch means
I love you!

A back stretch
does, too.

While ears
at attention!

Tail high!

Elbows low!

Can mean **Here come** . . . .

Belly up, tongue lolling,
an open-mouth grin?

Let's trade places and
wrestle again!

Tongue flick, sniff,
shake, shake, shake

says,

This game's too much.

Let's take a break.

Time for some **scritches?**

That's what people do
to say to a pupper,

I love
you, too!

Author's Note

Humans have thousands of words to communicate meaning. Dogs use their voices, too, but much of their communication is through body language.

Dogs' faces and tails give us lots of information, but to understand what a dog is *really* saying, you must look at their whole body and consider where they are and what is happening.

Just as some of the words we use can have more than one meaning, a dog's signal can mean one thing when they are playing and another when meeting a new dog in the park.

Dogs dance whole sentences. This book is full of pictures of dogs speaking their secret language. They are even on the endpapers! After you read about the dog language in this book, go back and look at the pictures carefully. Can you figure out what each dog is saying?

THE DOG LANGUAGE IN THIS BOOK

Look away: A dog looking away can mean very different things. Dogs who are meeting for the first time will often look away from one another for just a moment with a relaxed body posture and a happy wag. They are saying, *I am not a threat. Let's meet!* But if a dog looks up and away with a tight body and tense tail, they are saying, *Move along, move along. I don't want to meet.* Your dog may turn their head away with their chin down when you fuss at them. They are saying, *Please calm down. You are being scary.*

Wide, swishing wag: Dogs say a lot of things with their tails. A wag that is high and stiff is not friendly. It could even be a threat. But a low, swishing, butt-wiggly wag is a *very* friendly way of saying hello! Some scientists think that when a dog wags their tail, they are fanning their scent—their dog name—out to dogs or people they are meeting.

Blinking eyes: A dog sometimes blinks in a way that means *I want to be buddies. Do you?* Blinking is usually friendly and nice. When dogs want to look at each other, they might blink to show it is not a challenging stare.

Butt sniff: Humans may think it's odd when dogs sniff butts, but it is very important to dogs. It is how they find out whether their new dog friend is a male or female, how old they are, even how they are feeling. After dogs politely sniff one another's butts, they will sniff muzzles and ears. So much to learn!

Pee-mail?: Dogs pee on specific spots along pathways used by other dogs. You might see a dog stop and sniff, then leave a little pee of their own. They are leaving information that another dog's nose can "read," but are they intentionally leaving messages for other dogs? We don't know. Scientists are still researching what kind of information dogs might be transmitting through their pee.

Stiff body and face, turning away: Any dog can get into trouble if people do not understand when the dog is asking to be left alone. There are some signals that mean a dog doesn't want to be friends at that moment. If a dog's face and body are stiff, it is a signal that they want to be left alone. If their ears are back or their head is turned away, it is a sign that the dog feels threatened or afraid. They want to be left alone. Never try to pet a dog who wants to be left alone!

Greeting stretch: Dogs might stretch out their front legs, their back legs, or both, but if a dog greets you with a stretch, they are giving you a special honor and saying, *I love you sooooo much!*

Yawn: Dogs yawn when they are sleepy. They can even catch yawns from people! You might try yawning when you are sleepy to see if your dog yawns back! Dogs also yawn to say, *I am a little worried about what is going on.* You might see your dog yawning at the vet, or if two people are arguing. If your dog is yawning in front of another dog, they might not want to play.

Scratching: Dogs scratch to scritch itches. But sometimes they scratch to say, *This situation is making me nervous.*

Play bow: Elbows down, tail up sometimes means *Let's play!* But some dogs will play bow before they explode into . . .

Zoomies: A sudden BURST of energy! Zoomies are a way for dogs to release energy or tension. Sometimes they happen after a bath or when a dog is released from a leash or let out of a car. Sometimes they are just for fun! They are always fast, fast, fast!

Belly up: When a pup rolls belly up, it can mean *Please don't hurt me!* But when puppers are playing, wiggly, and relaxed, it means *I trust you* or *This is fun!*

Grinning: When dogs are grinning or smiling with an open mouth, their teeth may show, but they don't mean to be scary. However, dogs also sometimes show teeth to say, *Leave me alone, I might bite.* How can you tell if a dog is grinning or wants to be left alone? Look at their whole body, ears, tail, and face! Remember, a dog who wants to be left alone will probably have a tense body. Their tail may be up or down—even wiggling in a tight wag—but, if the dog is tense, it is not a happy wag. Their face will be tense, too, like they are ready to fight.

Tongue flick: When a dog's tongue flicks their nose, they might be saying, *I am nervous,* or they might be asking a person or another dog to calm down.

Ground sniff: Dogs sniff the ground to explore smells. But they also use sniffing the ground to say, *I need some space,* to other dogs.

Shake off: You've probably seen a dog shake, shake, shake when they have too much water in their fur. Dogs shake off tension, too. They shake, shake, shake off too much excitement!

MORE FASCINATING FACTS ABOUT OUR BEST FRIENDS

Dogs don't see colors the way humans do. Some scientists believe dogs see the world the way we see it at twilight. People might feel sorry for dogs because they can't see a rainbow exactly the way we do—but if dogs knew about our noses, they might feel sorry for us!

Humans have five to six million olfactory receptors in their noses. Dogs have up to three hundred million! Some dogs can smell things buried underground, even things under many feet of water and mud!

Dogs can smell time. Scents fade as time passes. That's how a dog knows when to wait at the door for someone who comes home at the same time every day. Their scent has faded.

Dogs can smell your emotions. Pheromones are chemical messages that animals (including humans) produce. Humans produce pheromones when they feel emotions such as fear, anger, sadness, or love. Dogs have a special organ called the vomeronasal organ (VNO), under the bone that separates their nostrils from the roof of their mouth. The VNO detects pheromones. When dogs sniff or lick their noses, they bring molecules of pheromone to the VNO. Dogs can smell how happy or sad you are, and even how much you love them!

Dogs communicate with other dogs through smell. Dogs have glands that produce pheromones around their ears, their muzzle, the pads of their feet, and even between their toes. Special scent glands on each side of their butt produce a smell unique to each dog. Some scientists think this might be the dog's "signature smell"—their dog name.

Special thanks to Arie Deller, Certified Dog Obedience Instructor, and Karen B. London, PhD, Certified Applied Animal Behaviorist, for their insightful comments on this text as it was becoming a book. Any mistakes that have crept in are entirely my own.
—Kersten Hamilton

SELECT BIBLIOGRAPHY

Chin, Lili. *Doggie Language: A Dog Lover's Guide to Understanding Your Best Friend.* London: Summersdale, 2020.

Hirch, Andy. *Science Comics: Dogs: From Predator to Protector.* New York: First Second, 2017.

Horowitz, Alexandra. "How Do Dogs 'See' with Their Noses?" TED-Ed Animations. ed.ted.com/lessons/how-do-dogs-see-with-their-noses-alexandra-horowitz.